HL

Geoffrey Beene

Text by Brenda Cullerton

Foreword by Richard Martin
and Harold Koda

Harry N. Abrams, Inc., Publishers

Editor: Ruth A. Peltason
Designer: J. Abbott Miller, Design/Writing/Research, New York

Library of Congress Cataloging-in-Publication Data
Cullerton, Brenda.
Geoffrey Beene/text by Brenda Cullerton.
foreword by Richard Martin and Harold Koda.
p.   cm.
ISBN 0-8109-3141-9
1. Beene, Geoffrey. 2. Fashion designers — United States — Biography.
3. Costume design — United States — History — 20th century. I. Title.
TT505.B367C85   1995
746.9.2.092 — dc20   95-7848
[B]

Contents

Foreword

Geoffrey Beene is an artist. Likening himself to a runaway, Beene is no fugitive. His reticence in the system of fashion is both the prerogative of indisputable, consummate mastery and the disposition and integrity of an artistic talent. As intellectual exercise, Mr. Beene poses a cogent skepticism, yet he is one of the world's great visionaries, idealistic in his belief in clothing progress and, with it, human adaptation. He has never yielded his anatomy-student's zeal for the body, respecting its form and imagining its potential for movement with the eye of one who might otherwise direct movies or choreograph modern dance. He takes an ethnographer's practiced witness to modern women: his second-story view onto 57th Street is one of the best-observed sites in the world, its style pulse taken with periodic discrimination by Mr. Beene with no more than a spin in his chair.

Beene's work is driven by an unrelenting, forgiving, abiding optimism: an optimism and incorrigible faith that we associate with modernism. The inspiring enthusiasm that one feels on being sent by Mr. Beene to see an exhibition on high-technology textiles for use in outer space or on having his recommendation to a dress by Mainbocher is to know the endorsement and the ardor of the new and renewed. Fabrics and findings are not for Mr. Beene a matter of the usual sources: materials, closures, bondings, and seams are ready to be reinvented by Mr. Beene's immense, utopian imagination.

In Beene's work, the response to materials is a touchstone. He uses technology with a transforming ingenuity. Materials of the past are recontextual-ized and contemporary innovations are explored without prejudice and the limita-tions of inherited ideas. His recent infatuation with artificial horsehair is not a techno-artisan's ardor alone. Beene's spring-summer 1995 collection features this affinity for new textiles, a buoyancy applied to boleros of helix structure and the abstract perimeters of Mondrianesque planes of textile, granting both the great grid of abstraction and the lightness and flexure of the body.

His travel endorsements are no chamber-of-commerce subscriptions. His Santa Monica is his vision of a Seurat Sunday made lithe, American, and contemporary; Mr. Beene's Vienna is a conflation of Hapsburg past and protocol and the lyricism of a world both real and imagined in strutting horses, grand carriages, and modern vitality; Mr. Beene's Americana is whitewashed Emersonian saltbox framed by flora redolent of Victorian and Edwardian gardens;

his Hawaii is not simply the beach at Waikiki and the melting-pot beauty of the Islanders, but a Corbu edifice in tropical splendor — the Machine Age and Arcadia.

There is a quality of gladness to Mr. Beene's work that seldom occurs in contemporary culture. Not to be mistaken with ostentation or with purports of glamour, Beene's unabashed joyfulness is generated in such details as the surprising strength and elasticity of lace, the flex and bounce of bias horsehair tape, and the protean possibilities of wool jersey. Beene treats structural necessity with nonchalance when disposing geometry strategically on the human body. The tour-de-force simplicity of a double-faced coat is enough: Beene never trumps us into enforced hyperbole. There is charm and wit in the clothing. His irreverence and apostasy spice but never overwhelm a disciplined pragmatism. In a culture that calls attention to minor power and slight skills, Mr. Beene's work always possesses the generous gentlemanliness of a perfect resolution that seeks obscurity or, at most, reserved recognition.

It is important to realize that Mr. Beene's critical disbelief is possible only because of the unerring, positive faith of his work. Others yield to the Establishment out of anxiety regarding their own contribution or distinction. Beene's work is not fashion in any collective sense. It is not responsible to society at large nor to the composite mood of the moment. The definite, personal style of Beene is never contingent. It possesses art's condition of being unconditional. Beene is a master, an artist of no measure or peer among others in his aesthetic practice.

There is a privilege throughout this book in hearing Mr. Beene's voice in complement to his aesthetic achievement. What he, in his modesty, will never say is that we, all who follow his work, are privileged to know fashion's persistent quest and personal genius for our time.

Richard Martin and Harold Koda

To the reader / viewer

How exactly does a dress spring from fiction onto flesh? When does the idea first take flight? Does it begin with some spasm or surfeit of light? A jolt like two wires crossed spitting sparks? Does the idea come out of nowhere? Everywhere? From isolation? Desolation? Exposure?

Even on an inanimate dummy, the "body" beneath this dress would move a man. It isn't that there's much to see. A bit of the shoulder and back, the sudden suggestion of leg. But what the naked eye can't see, the mind's eye is free and forced to explore. What exquisitely painful pleasures, what infinitely intriguing possibilities, lie within this liberated and captive state.

As for the woman who slips into its caress . . . the fact that it is so inexplicably simple; that there are no buttons, no zippers, and just a single seam; the fact that it is cut from less than 4 1/2 feet of feather–light fabric and feels like nothing on, is almost immaterial. Unconstricted by the conventional mechanics of dress, she, too, is liberated. Far from an object that is subject to others' desires, she is at the mercy of only her own.

Giving a woman the means to make the most (or the least) of those desires is what motivates Geoffrey Beene. How it happens or why isn't his concern. "The mystery and the magic for me," he says "is that it happens at all." This book makes no attempt to solve the mystery. It merely acknowledges its presence.

The Presence of Absence

"Nothingness is everything," declares fashion's resident alien, the happy heretic Geoffrey Beene. While people on the Manhattan street below race for cabs and buses in the pouring rain, he bunches some precious bit of lace into a ball, then cajoles it onto the arms of a mannequin. The gesture is so familiar it should have a patent pending. Nevertheless, what a moment ago you assumed was nothing more than a fragment of fabric, a handkerchief, suddenly becomes a bolero. "You see, it's barely there," whispers Beene, "Beauty and the least."

The moment teaches the novice two fundamental facts about this "lesson in perplexity" known as Mr. Beene. The first is that to assume anything about the man or his work is to presume. Presumption violates his cherished laws of propriety. Because it implies a lack of respect, it isn't fitting. Period. Second is the fact that whether you're looking at a gown created from 38 yards of silk chiffon, a dress cut from one yard of wool jersey, or a life — his life — the presence of absence is key.

He attributes it to the creative "process of elimination." But there is more to it than what is missing from a jersey dress: the buttons, the zipper, the seams. Consider, for instance, what has been eliminated from a cover story on him in the magazine Louisiana Life. It was recently unearthed from his archives on 7th Avenue. "Louisiana Born. Fashion Bred" announces the innocuous headline written back in 1989. Within the body of this piece, a piece which celebrates the triumphs of a long gone, albeit, native son, there are several scalpel-like incisions. Deliberate cuts made with a razor that remove a sentence, a caption, even a short paragraph. It is like that piece of lace. The holes hint at the significance of what is hidden. They inspire an exaggerated desire to know and to see just a little more. In that sense, they reveal as much about the man and his work as they conceal.

Control is crucial. Beene is as meticulous in the construction of the memories and myths that create his image as he is in that of his clothing. Any attempt to fill in the blanks is met with testy impatience. "May I remind you this is a book about my work. Not some Vanity Fair whodunit!" he faxes one summer afternoon. "Clarity not intrigue should win out." In the same vein and later that summer: "Communication is part of what is accomplished with clothing. What is made of it, what it is turned into after it leaves the designer's hands, there is the connection of who is there."

For the man who is there in the meantime, the connection is long distance; riddled with contradictions and that occasional burst of static. Even his relaxed appearance is deceiving: the unconstructed jacket, the banded collar shirt, the slippers. It is a uniform that other designers have only recently "discovered" in menswear and that he has been wearing since 1978. It is the very essence of comfort and ease. Yet he is a singularly uneasy and formal man. Rumor and press indicate that he is "shy," "arrogant," "charming," "ornery," "respectful," "radical," "difficult," "generous," "perverse," "impish". . . .

He is. But no amount of press quite prepares one for the manner in which he conducts a conversation. It, too, is shocking in its formality. "I would not wish it." "I did not think it." "I can not tolerate it." The language is exceedingly polite and, like his work, precise. It has nothing whatever to do with what is casual. There are no short cuts. No abbreviations or contractions. Like some strange vestigial limb, it speaks of those distant but ever-present Southern origins.

Archaic and quaint as it might sound, there is no doubt, however, that it is a language born of conviction. Perhaps it's no coincidence when Grace Mirabella says, "The marvel of Geoffrey Beene's clothing is that it makes you move with the comfort of conviction." Convictions have always been incompatible with the short-lived ins and outs, the news and nows, of fashion. They are a source of those irreconcilable differences, the beloved contradictions which compel him.

What Sylvia Plath called "The magnificence of the mysterious" also compels him. That magnificence applies to everything from beauty, which he defines as "a measure of energy," to the revelation of touching and working with a piece of fabric that he's been on intimate terms with for over thirty years only to discover it is still an unknown. "It's like someone who speaks the English language and who through use becomes a poet," says Harold Koda, a curator at The Metropolitan Museum of Art's Costume Institute. "His affinity, his exploration of the abstraction of cloth, has allowed him to push its possibilities in ways that are unimaginable."

The "magnificence of the mysterious." It is the act of surrendering to the unforeseen. It is the reason he dresses a woman. Beene is a former medical student who gave up the scalpel for a pair of scissors over forty-five years ago. Since that time, he has filled literally hundreds of press books with his thoughts about women. He describes himself as a reluctant "prodder," a "provoker." (Within the bounds of propriety, of course.) His business, his work, depends on anticipating not only the practical needs of a woman but on what one loyal client and friend calls "the unspoken ambitions, the unvoiced longings" as well.

27

This is the inner life which must find expression in the form of his clothing. Adept as he is in both analyzing and animating the echo of that inner life, the very idea of dissecting his own is as much an anathema as that fateful afternoon he first confronted a human cadaver at Tulane. "I'm happy knowing as little about myself as I do," he confesses. "Knowing more might harm me."

Geoffrey Beene. Barely There. Dialogue with Shadows. Obviously NOT. Highly Charged. Body Guarded. These are just a few of the titles he suggested and dismissed before tentatively settling on Flight Patterns. For the man who has never stopped moving and the era he inhabits, it seemed perfect. It was also torture. A title automatically implies that something is final. Finished. Beene is rarely, if ever, content with what is done. He does not wish to settle. He is a pioneer.

From today's psychologically correct point of view, Daniel Boone himself would probably be defined not as a pioneer but as a severely dysfunctional human being whose unresolved conflicts with authority figures made him a compulsive risk taker. But where would America's settlers have been without him?

Pioneers are those who must be where others are not. They do not compromise. They do not conform. To conform to the demands of this age of so-called instant access—an age obsessed by the need to know it all and to tell it all, too—is out of the question for Beene. Others may choose to bare their logo'ed souls on TV talk shows or to cocoon into homes as safe as security systems can make them. He prefers to be out there. In touch but untouchable.

For him, it is the familiar which is unfamiliar. He seeks out and exalts in all that is left of the world's impenetrable spaces. Those spaces include privacy (a new unknown for some, but an old friend to Beene), countries such as Japan and China, a city like Vienna, women, and the future. It's all virgin territory. It moves him.

No, he isn't plugged in, jacked up, wired. Much as he loves the idea of technology, of this final frontier, he admits that he can not even focus his television. He refers to video as the "vee-day-oh," a photo copier as the "cope-e-ay." As for the phone, he can pick it up and hang up. The options in between utterly

confound him. Yet, the single adjective most often used to describe this man is and has always been "modern."

How ironic that the long-buried roots in rural Louisiana are not modern at all. Here, where a sense of place and knowing one's place, where who you were, not what you did, determined who you would be, Beene's future as a rebel and frequent flyer became a fait accompli. Despite the Southern accent, he is not a man who whistles Dixie, either in his cups or under his breath. His absence from this once-upon-a-time land of magnolias, cotton, (and rampant contradictions) has done little to make his heart grow fonder of it.

His maternal grandfather was the town doctor. Two of his grandfather's sons were also doctors. Mr. Beene's mother wished the same for her son. Everyone who has followed his career has heard the stories. He painted the rooms of his house a different color on weekends. He bought the Bristol blue, white, and orange polka dot cloth at a local 5 & 10 and had his aunt sew up a pair of beach pajamas from a store-bought pattern. These are public domain—stock photos. Much as he loathes looking back, when he does flex the muscles of memory, the recollections are as loosely but brilliantly drawn as one of his free-form sketches.

There is the sketch of a black "manservant" leading him on a walk through his grandfather's plantation. "I must have been five or six. There were the cows and livestock and the scuppernong vines trailing over the arbor. It was immaculately clean and everything was in its proper place. Most thoughtfully, all the hens were in their little nests in the shade of a chinaberry tree. The man wanted me to touch one, to feel the egg and the hen's down. I was terrified of the beak and all that pecking. But I did it. And I realized this was my first reach into sensuality. Because the eggs were warm. It was the shape and hardness—the softness—of the feathers, all at the same time. I was frozen with the sensation."

As he wanders through those vacant rooms of childhood, he also sees the color red: "The vivid red of my mother's lipstick. I was a small child, staring up at her in a cane chair. It was a rocking chair. The lips were big, like a Dali painting." And his grandmother's attic: "All the prints. The Victorianism. I always found it enchanting. The underside of wooden chairs, the decorative boxes and chests, they were covered inside and out with floral-sprigged fabric. I've been infatuated with boxes all my life. When you open them you never know what's hiding inside. It's the unknown. They are perfect even when they are empty."

This is a glimpse of the South Beene eventually fled, the South he says he is still fleeing. Fossilized in his memory, it feels as remote as the Jurassic period. But no woman who has ever stepped into his garments is a stranger to it: a rich Venetian silk velvet dress innerlined with a provincial print in wool challis, an eighteenth-century bow sewn inside a vest, an inset of black point d'esprit with the pulse of an embroidered heart at its center, a pair of snow-white cotton and red satin piped gloves. This is the kind of rarefied elegance which must be extinct. It is out of place in the new and the now and belongs back in the days of the Marquis de Custine, when "the duty of an empress was to amuse herself to death."

Or does it? When Beene says, as he did in 1963, that he "worships" women, that he "glorifies" them, when he says again as recently as 1992, "I think of a woman as a flower . . . fragile, vulnerable and an object of beauty and desire," the reflex response of a "liberated" woman is, "This man is out of his mind. He's a dinosaur." Yet, an indefinable something hits home.

"The epic longing to be more than we are." This is how Seymour Krim sums up the uniqueness of the American spirit. Thanks to that hunger, that craving, Americans are forever reaching forward. For us, the habit and what Krim dubs "the spaciousness of hope" resides not in the past — not in our rich or humble beginnings — but in the future. Whatever is lost in that stretch, the struggle to gain new ground, is forgotten. It's put behind us. If the past nips, even bites us in our joggers' heels, we run a little faster.

The American women's movement and Beene's lifework have been defined by that same exhilaration — the sensation of breaking free. "Beene works a bias so finely around bodily curves," raved an ecstatic reviewer after his fall 1994 show, "that even his seams look like they're picking up speed."

In that show on an overcast Monday morning, Beene had sent a troupe of modern dancers and models out onto a New York stage. He and his choreographer showed them leaping for the sky, doing grand jetés in layers of weightless wool melton, jersey, mohair, and silk matelassé. Here was a vision that shed a new and noble light on the meaning of upward mobility. Despite the darkened stage, the message was clear. This was a designer who understood and reveled in that irresistible yearning not to have but to be more.

Beene invites a woman to spread her wings. He also brings her gently down to earth. His clothing functions. It dances. It resurrects some part of the ritual once associated with dress, the ceremony which accompanied a transformation. It isn't that one has to summon a servant to fasten hundreds of buttons or pull on the strings of a whalebone corset. The jumpsuit, his self-ordained "ballgown of the 21st century," a "working uniform," slips on as effortlessly as a pair of jeans and a tee-shirt. (Unfortunately, it costs slightly more.)

But in handling a woman with such care, in taking the time to create something that dazzles the eye and sits against the skin as softly and exquisitely as that hen's down, he stays true to his promise. He does glorify her. For one splendid moment, the moment when she lingers and looks in the mirror, when she sees herself reflected in the eyes of others or soaring for the sky on a shadowlit stage, she feels more than just human.

She feels the tiniest bit divine. The Divinity within—home of his "angels," "goddesses," "saints," and "sinners." There is enormous courage, comfort, and joy in this sacred space. Enough to abandon fear and one's own cocoon; enough to face the world with the force of one's own passions — with "conviction," as Mirabella points out.

"Clothing must anticipate a woman's every move," he said in 1977. "It must never, ever hold her back." This is the reality that establishes an everyday context for Beene's fantasies. "The flight of art has to find its counterpart in the domain of the everyday, just as the condor casts its shadow on the ground," scrawled Polish writer Witold Gombrowicz in his Diary. It is this context which gives much of Beene's work such infinite relevance. Yes, he recognizes a woman's need to be strong, defiant, equal not elevated. But in the accelerated rush of departure, he also notes that the destination is as elusive as ever. What better, what more logical reason for him to attempt to bewitch and enthrall us — to dress us as a 1994 issue of French Vogue suggests: "in dreams, in wonder, in mystery, in space."

"The distinctive quality of Geoffrey Beene's work which at the same time reflects an immediate sensuous response to the color and texture of beautiful fabrics must be characterized as a variety of intellectualism," noted Kennedy Fraser in a 1977 New Yorker piece. "His brand of thoughtfulness goes beyond semantic dabblings and historic parlor games. It is a sincerely reflective response to women's image of themselves and to the society in which they live." Seven years later, fashion historian and photo journalist Bill Cunningham would observe that, "His credo is an island of stability and a respecter of precedence . . . He is an astute connoisseur of human vanity."

Vanity and respect: "Respect for the body, respect for the fabric, respect for a woman's desires." These are constants for the unruly Beene. Others inflate the newfound virtues of pared-down necessities, a wardrobe of five easy pieces, while he himself waxes poetic about the "the brilliance of America's original uniform: the sweatshirt, baggy chinos, and sneakers." Yet his concept of basics goes back further than that. It goes all the way back to his own impenetrable spaces: to those spaces found on pages 110 and 479 in his premed textbook, Gray's Anatomy. The heart, the mind.

This is the universe he is out to seduce and to conquer. It is a universe where there are no boundaries and for which there are still no maps. It is here where hope, faith, and awe find their future. The beauty, the wonder of it is that no machine, no computer, no matter how sophisticated, with or without a million gigabytes, rams, roms, peripherals, or windows, will ever contain or fathom its complexities. "I never in my life thought a woman was simple," he says. "Maybe

it is that mystery that is the challenge of dressing and identifying her. It is the charm and the attraction, too . . . ."

There are moments when the mystery assumes bizarre dimensions. Dimensions which open a small window into the soul of this sometimes gentle man. The film 30, which director Tom Kalin produced in honor of Beene's 30 years at work, is one such example. "The clothes will be contextualized," explained Kalin in a interview with Elle in 1993. "We'll show what it means to live in them, weep in them, to get snowed on. This is not about how elegant clothes can look when they're catwalked and spotlit."

Obviously NOT. 30 is shot entirely in black and white and in the eerie half light of what looks like a solar eclipse. As a far-from-weightless journey into the realms of death and desire, it pays homage to Beene's love of the Grand Guignol, to the grandeur of the void. The decaying French château with its maze of formal gardens is a spectacular backdrop for the Beene-dressed bodies who glide along a receiving line bussing the air before embracing impending chaos. As you rewind and fast forward, you freeze-frame on the howl of a hideous, cronelike woman, the froideur of a young goddess married to a portrait of her own avarice: the aging and decadent older man and the doomed male lover. As the emotional seams unravel, you feel as if you're traveling into some polar region of extremes — a frigid place where beauty has an expiration date clearly marked on the silk, lace, satin, tulle, and jersey wrappings.

This is not your typical fashion video. The clothes play only a cameo role. But in its dissonance, its contradictions, it features more than a few of Beene's favorite things. It jars the eye. It forces one to refocus. "What I loved about it was that he allowed it to be done," says Koda. "No matter what it responded to, it was a revelation on some level of what he wanted. . . ."

"Indeed, indeed," as Mr. Beene would say. Whether the film was understood or appreciated by those who viewed it is irrelevant. Like the 1994 dance performance and the countless confrontations with the unpredictable that make the man and his work so hard to pin down, it was an invitation to surrender to the unforeseen. Yet another form of protest from the master of propriety — from the man who has rarely fit in but always stood out.

"New legislation is being pushed through at high speeds for the isolation of all you 'don't fitter inners' and that word 'isolation' can mean several things, none of which things is pleasant for the isolated individual."

It was Tennessee Williams who put these words into the mouth of a petty power mongerer named Braden in his short story, "The Knightly Quest." Braden is speaking to his brother, Gewinner, a man who has returned from a life abroad only to find his small town overrun by some faceless, omnipotent entity called The Project. The Project is Geoffrey Beene's bogeyman. It is the system, any system, which condemns an individual to live by the rules he abhors: "Rules which have significance only to the people who make them. I like the fact that my clothing doesn't fit in with other stories; that the collections don't fit with what others are espousing. The purpose of design is to assert whatever creative energies and talents I may have as an individual."

This statement ran in Detour magazine twenty-eight years after his "birth" announcement in Women's Wear Daily on May 10, 1963. Even a brief trip through those early years via fashion's headlines gives one some idea of the

distance traveled. In retrospect, the headlines foreshadowed the future of a man whose convictions emerged from contradiction and whose presence even then was best defined by his absence.

"Dare to Wear Pants!" "Mini Takes All!" "Braless Movement Sweeping Nation." They are essentially prehistoric. For some women, they marked the beginnings of a euphoric joyride; a full-scale revolution against the very rules Beene contests. For Beene himself, however, they are not unlike the flashbacks suffered on some hallucinogenic drug. As he confirms in a 1993 issue of Interview: "Freedom meant so much then that too many liberties were taken." His acid reaction to the tyranny of trend, to the dictates of anti-establishment fashion were as bold as his brilliant but archly conservative bias-cut dresses.

"Enter Geoffrey Beene. Brimming Over with a Spirited Image," proclaimed that first announcement in Women's Wear, the very same paper which would purge him from its pages in 1983. This soon-to-be bastion of fashion was welcoming one of America's first designer-driven companies. "Up until now, it has been the manufacturer's image," explained Beene at the time. "With limitations and restrictions imposed . . . Now, I have greater freedom, no restrictions whatsoever. No such thing as repeating last season's dress—which I loathe."

"The daredevil of young couture." "A pacesetter." "Geoffrey Beene has Flair!" "Beene Stalk Blooms!" He was an overnight sensation in newspapers everywhere from New York and Chicago to Biloxi and Indianapolis. "Suburban matrons looking for oomph," "fun-loving sophisticates," and "women on the go" . . . . They all loved him.

In his first spring collection, critics applauded many of the same elements

which to this day are synonymous with Beene: In the words of the Dallas Times Herald: "There was gingham, like a tablecloth, embroidered with the surprise of henna sequins," pinstripes, progressive polka dots, his cut on the bias, and one dress in particular, "The Brushstroke." "Here within the framework of a lean supple streak of a dress," reported the paper, "he has created real fashion excitement because when he couldn't find a fabric he wanted, he invented it himself."

While First and lesser ladies sipped tea and cocktails in their Beene creations, younger women howled for more of the Fab Four on the Ed Sullivan show. "I adore the Beatles but I do not have to dress their followers," came the tart response from the "unassuming and bespectacled" designer. Those followers might dance the Funky Chicken, the Frug, and the Watusi, but not in the exquisitely constructed suits, reversible coats, and "demure little frocks" he made for their mothers.

There would be no topless bathing suits à la Rudi Gernreich, no naked models with shaved eyebrows parading down his runways. "I'm revolting against the way magazines are suggesting a woman dress. They have reached the ultimate in bad taste. I'd hate to see future historians refer to us as the Barbarians of the 60s."

He now dismisses much of this period's work as "uptight little dresses which hid all my misgivings"; dresses which his 25th retrospective catalogue aptly describe as "Superstructures." "They were so stiff they could stand up by themselves," he says. But they were a form of genuflection. A tribute to all that he had learned (and would later "unlearn") at the knee of French couture.

Like many Americans who make that first pilgrimage of youth to Paris, this was the city where he saw the light. "My life began there. It began the moment people understood what I wanted to do." Commuting between an unheated villa in St. Germain en Laye and a maid's garret in the city ("Bathing once a week for a Virgo wasn't very amusing, believe me"), he apprenticed with a tailor who had once worked for the great Irish cum French couturier, Captain Edward Molyneux. He sketched at L'Academie Julian. He attended his first Elsa Schiaparelli couture show. In abandoning the familiarity of his mother tongue and the life of a "don't fitter inner" par excellence, Beene immersed himself in the language of his craft. It was a language which would deliver him from exile and bring him "home," at last. Home to his work — the only place in the world where he would ever feel truly rooted. In beginning to master the mechanics of dress, he was about to set the mysterious free.

In those first five years of business (nearly twelve years after he had returned from Paris and served time on Seventh Avenue), he won three of his eight Coty Awards to come (one of his industry's most prestigious tokens of acclaim). Jean Shrimpton appeared on the cover of Vogue in Beene. And President Johnson's daughter, Lynda Bird, chose him to design her wedding dress. While American bombers were blowing up North Vietnamese air bases and Martin Luther King, Jr., led freedom marchers through Selma, Alabama, fashion's head-lines went wild. "Beene Won't Talk," "Beene Keeps Wrap on Gown!" "Med School Dropout Designing Works for Lynda!" In refusing to reveal even the scantiest details to Women's Wear, "That Dress," as the paper dubbed it, became a sort of symbol. Like the dragon's teeth in the Greek myth, it would sow the seeds of his oh-so-civil wars against the powers that be.

But going against the grain came naturally to Geoffrey Beene. He was all about bias. To keep the world on its toes, he gladly turned assumption on its head. In 1968, the same year Lynda Bird walked down the aisle to marry Capt. Charles Robb in her $2,000 princess gown, he sent the famous sequined football jersey out into America's ballrooms. Two years previously, he had transformed menswear's own grey flannel and wool jersey into dresses that the most staid of socialites happily danced the Pony not to mention the waltz in. Denim and sweat-shirting would soon follow on their stilettoed heels.

This is the Beene we recognize in the current retrospectives. These dresses were exceptions to the early rules. But they set an almighty precedent. A precedent which might make "Pioneer" the most appropriate occupation listed in his dog-eared passport. From the day he opened his own company in 1963, to 1971 when he introduced Beenebag, one of America's first secondary lines, and beyond—straight through to the nineties when he deserted fashion's mega-modeled runways in favor of stationary installations and theatrical performances, Beene has been flying against the face of fashion's conventions. A flesh and blood version of the Stealth Bomber.

There have been the occasional crash landings. Licensing deals gone awry. The demise of Beenebag. The failure of perfumes such as Geoffrey Beene and Red. There have even been moments when he stooped to conquer. (The mention of an appearance on the TV show "Love Boat" still makes him wince.) But creatively, most of the failures eventually became glorious accidents.

There is no question that he is a man of extremes. He "loves," he "loathes" with few "Mickey Mouse euphemisms" in between. He is as proud as he is prejudiced. "The South has been greatly misunderstood," he says one morning. What he neglects to add is the fact, the feeling, that he, too, has suffered from similar "misunderstandings" (a euphemism). In 1978, two years after he had packed up his collection and flown off to show it in Milan—an unheard of move for an American, in which he literally went for broke, borrowing every cent it took from a bank—he explained the impulse to a New York journalist: "I thought if they couldn't understand me at home, maybe they would on another continent."

Such sentiments are usually his best-kept secrets. They form the ambivalent terrain of his memories. Indeed, of his wounds. Wounds which the distance of time has done little to heal. Like most human beings, he is the sum of his secrets, his silence, and his losses. As his clothing proves, however, he is also a human being who has managed to transform the weight, the sum of those losses, into an uncanny state of weightlessness and grace.

"Alone in his glory," "outside the mainstream mold," "a one-man band," "pays no obeisance to" . . . . This is how reviewers have come to terms with the presence of his absence; with his merciless pursuit of perfection and independence. Just as that same independence has isolated him as an individual

but liberated him as an artist, his pursuit of perfection has made him his own most lethal opponent. Whatever punishments the system (or Tennessee William's so-called Project) may have in store for him, it will undoubtedly be his pleasure to endure.

In the meantime, he continues to struggle with oblivion — with the nothingness (and the traditions) from which all real art evolves. Within that

vacuum, he is perpetually at risk, a prime mover. He cannot stop. Not anymore than a jetliner can turn off its engines in mid-flight. Even physically, he can't bear standing still.

He regrets the mediocrity of the present. As he has in the past, he looks forward only to the future. (A future in which collars, linings, lapels, buttons, padding, zippers, and seams will all be history.) For the moment, however, Geoffrey Beene is like some nomad dancing on the head of his pins. A man who appears destined to function forever in and out of time. It is for this reason, perhaps, that his clothing enjoys a form of everlasting life.

Conflict with Interest

"Where else does the impossible swallow the inconceivable on a daily basis?"

H. L. Mencken was speaking of American politics, not fashion, when he posed that question fifty years ago. He could just as easily have been sitting in a back-row seat at a Geoffrey Beene show with the Cleveland Plain Dealer in 1987. "In the hands of a less adept designer," remarked the reviewer about Beene's own upcoming version of "the impossible swallowing the inconceivable," "a collection that encompasses everything from bedspread chenille and gold spattered faille or silver leather to monk's cloth would be a nightmare."

Horsehair and gazar. Rubies with rope. Mattress ticking and sequins. Lace and leather. Silk tulle and straw. Men's shirting and chiffon. These are merely a few of the confounding combinations Beene has conjured up over the years. Richard Martin, in his essay on Beene's wit in the catalogue Unbound, refers to them as "indiscreet liaisons." Yet what might be considered an unholy alliance for some is a marriage made in heaven for Beene. (If he believed in heaven, which as a lapsed Baptist whose ears once burned hearing about the fires of hell, he probably does not.)

In any case, he delights in pulling the proverbial wool (lined with satin) over unsuspecting eyes. In pairing the sturdiest tweed with the flimsiest lace, in covering the opaque surface of apple-green mohair with hundreds and hundreds of handsewn, translucent pailletes, and in pulling out all the stops with industrial zippers and plastic tubing. As always, however, there is a method to his madness, an irrefutable logic behind the magic.

Beene calls it "Alchemy. In elevating the humblest fabrics, in making them as luxurious and as desirable as the richest, I create a new context for both. I remove the stigmas attached to them." In Webster's dictionary, a stigma is "a mark of shame or discredit." In Beene's world, it is grounds for immediate dismissal, expulsion.

It's ironic. For hundreds of years European sumptuary laws restricted the use of his luxurious fabrics — of silks, velvet, lace, and furs — to the nobility. It was a means of keeping people in their proper place, an early form of "station identification." In his radical revision of those laws, Geoffrey Beene, the All-American, indulges in an act of perfectly civil disobedience. He does an about-face akin to the creation of his reversible fabrics. In removing the stigmas, he turns irony into wit and beauty.

He has always used the noblest fabrics; those which he confesses are "so exquisite, it's blasphemy to cut into them." So exquisite, says British Vogue, "his heart bleeds" when he sharpens his scissors. They are his "inspiration." But they are rarely alone, rarely divorced from the commoner's favorites: from ginghams, grey flannels, mattress ticking, cotton piqués, and wool jersey. "If I worked in nothing but wool jersey, I'd be happy," he claims. "It's so forgiving . . . You can tailor it, drape it, stretch it, shape it . . . ." Within this conflict, a conflict that resolves itself so blissfully in the details, lies interest and a deeper truth about Beene, the man and artist.

Although the unlikely marriage between rich and humble had always existed, the first use of the terminology was in 1977. After his fall show, Kennedy Fraser informed New Yorker readers that "other designers showed flashy furs and metallic fabrics that throbbed like Times Square neon with information about their cost. But when Beene showed a luxurious-looking coat with deep sable cuffs, the coat itself was made of a relatively humble chocolate-colored corduroy."

Fraser's remark may have hit closer to home than even Beene imagines. In his open-hearted appreciation of the lesser stuff, there may be some of his expatriate Southern soul showing through. Florence King, in her book Southern Ladies and Gentlemen, talks of "the quick Southern instinct that can spot the one illiterate mountaineer out of a hundred who possesses an elusive quality of homespun grace. He is a gentleman," she adds. "And that's that. The rich, vulgar man is not." In this same paragraph, she also talks of the Southerner's adulation of "those invisible, inborn traits that mark the aristocrat of the spirit."

An aristocrat in the true sense of the word is somebody so comfortable in his or her own skin, so remarkably self-possessed, they are able not only to move virtually anywhere with disarming ease but to put the world around them at ease. Stripped of the status symbols and social airs which serve only to belittle one's

authentic self, the aristocrat is one of the very few who understands the nature and the power of "nothingness," of sumptuous simplicity.

Sumptuous simplicity. It is an aristocratic ideal for the democratic Mr. Beene. An ideal which ironically enough has as much to do with the "homespun grace" of Florence King's "illiterate mountaineer" as it does with the haughty elite of Europe's upper classes. With the emergence of a nouveau riche middle class in the nineteenth century, aristocrats sought a novel, new means of retaining their niche. Simplicity was it.

As Phillipe Perrot relates in Fashioning the Bourgeoisie, his study of clothing in that century, "Simplicity opposed pretensions, fads, and affectations thus acquiring its value. It assumed different forms and content but remained the main barrier and standard that revealed class distinctions." In citing this example, "It is poor women who have to put on all their finery for the grand soiree. Only the immensely wealthy can afford to be excessively simple," he fast-forwards straight into Beene's own twentieth-century ballrooms and corporate boardrooms.

In simplicity is stability. The gulf between the woman who can afford it and the woman who cannot marks the difference between one who struggles to fit into the "latest" style and one who simply possesses it. For that woman, Beene invents some of the most fabulously complex and costly fabrics on earth. His clothing is so intricately constructed only those who create them can alter them. They are, as he so triumphantly attests, "uncopyable." But it is his simplicity (simplicity so startling, so elegant, that actress Glenn Close remembers turning down an offer to wear Harry Winston's precious jewels at the 1989 Oscars because "Beene's finished dress, the shrug as he called it, just didn't need them") that embodies the most spectacularly mysterious example of "the impossible swallowing the inconceivable."

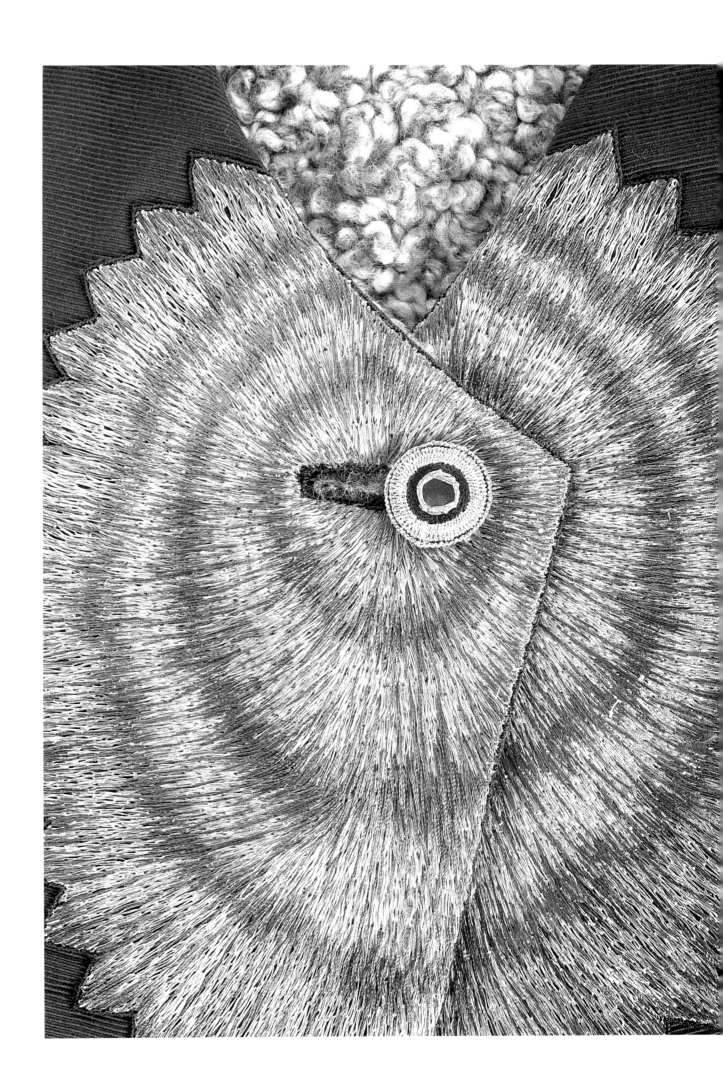

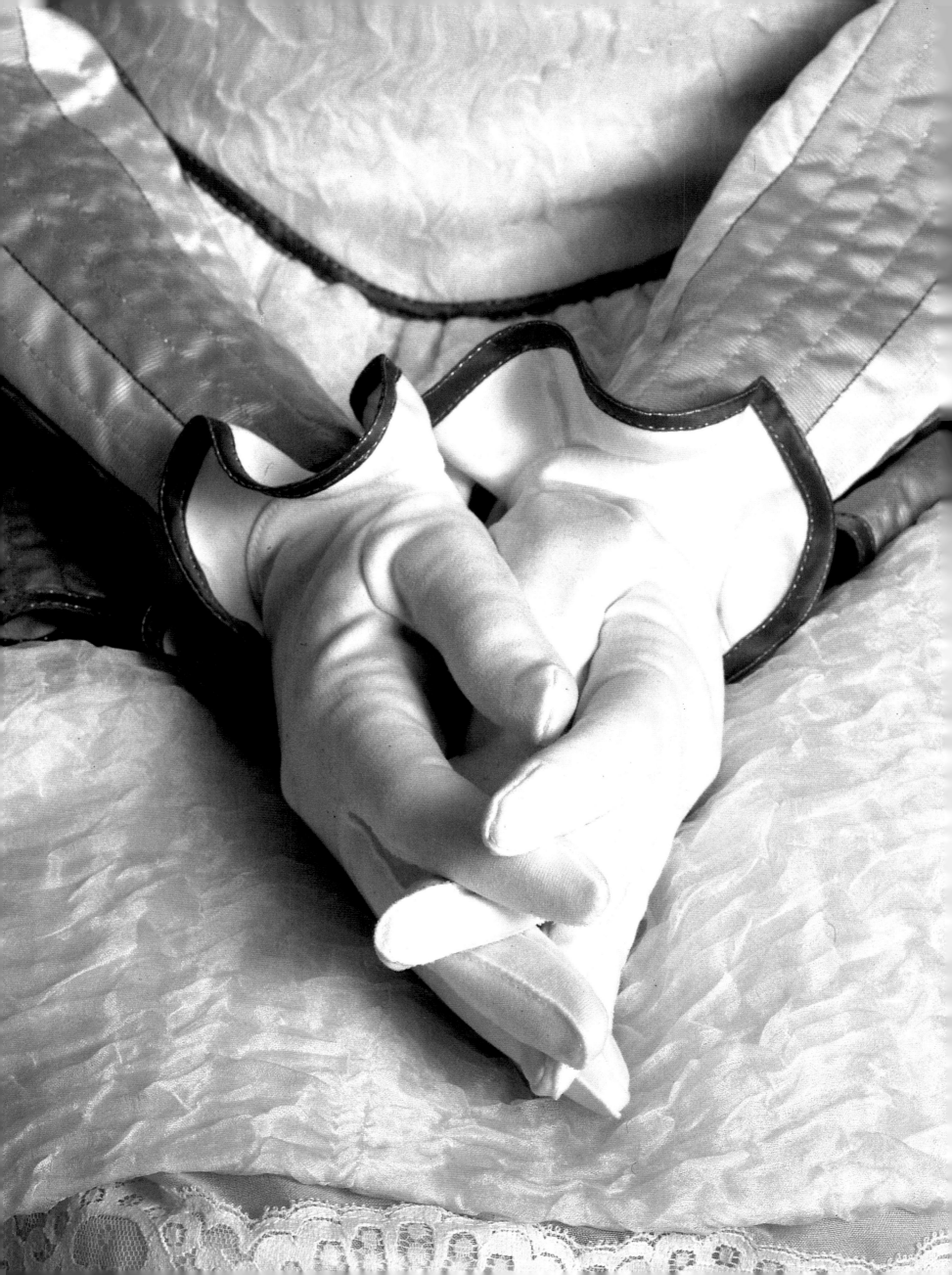

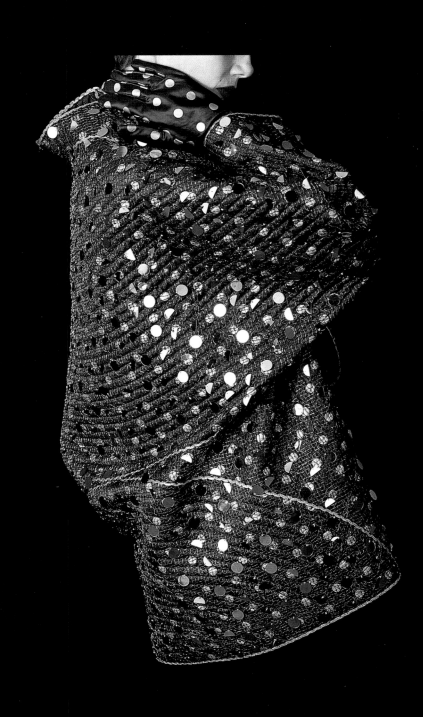

Frequent Flying

"His reverie was not simply a reverie of escape. It was a reverie of flight."
Gaston Bachelard, The Poetics of Reverie

Who are the frequent flyers in Geoffrey Beene's extraterrestrial (and celestial) world? They are women who fly not on gossamer wings but on wings made of quilted gold satin. They dress in clothing that weighs less than a zipper and fits in the palm of the hand. They never use hangers. ("Hangers are the most archaic aspect of our culture," says Beene.) They pack a single bag and travel everywhere from Borneo to Bimini. Unlike women who lug along emotional baggage and live in perpetual fear of losing their Samsonite, one fantasizes that these freely moving bodies are the first of their species to experience the bliss and the rapture of "the unfettered self."

In Mary Gordon's book of ferociously lucid essays, Good Boys and Dead Girls, the author identifies the real and the mythical American male in terms of this "search for the unfettered self." She reminds the reader that women are the ties, the fetters, that slow a man down. In order to fulfill his destiny, he must, by necessity, become rootless and leave them behind.

In Beene's present and future world, women are not rootless. They belong. Yet they are also unbound. They share that same lust for the giddiness and the grace of flight. "Rippling slivers of leather," "seams radiating from the chest, streaming down the sleeves," "aerodynamic quilting . . . holding the head aloft," "sinuous triangles (that) evoke images of . . . Brancusi's Birds In Space." When journalist Amy Fine Collins (a woman many claim to be Beene's muse) describes Beene's 1990 fall collection, even words have wings.

The fact that these women cannot literally fly is moot. They move. And of course, they dance. Their "split leaps and pirouettes," their "bending," "stretching," and "twirling," their spins in space are far from yet another form of grueling exercise. They express a need to defy the gravity of twentieth-century lives. Lives, which though self-propelled, are occasionally grounded by soaring

ambition; lives, which though liberated, also carry the weight of untold doubts and responsibility. Thanks to Beene's imagination and to his creative "process of elimination," these women bear the burden of freedom as lightly as his layerings of tweed, even vinyl and chiffon.

Like Beene, they are also women who consider humor a form of flight: levitation. A fat little king, Felix the Cat, a big red Stop sign on the front of a fancy ballgown. It's like turning a collar in front into suspenders in the back, implying nudity when there is none. It isn't that he is making fun. It's a gentle ribbing. Like the shimmering satin skeleton on the front of yet another dancing dress.

In speaking with Beene, one discovers a man who appreciates a gentle ribbing, too. It is only when this teasing, which treads the tightrope between tension and truth, accidentally stumbles into his "No Trespassing" zone that one's wings are instantly clipped. Otherwise, there are no paralyzing categories, no borders that limit the expansiveness of a woman's horizons.

As David Livingstone confirms in The Toronto Globe and Mail in 1994, "Not only has he proved that even the prettiest clothes need not be any impediment to the full expression of muscle and limb, he has also dissolved the borders between playing field and ballroom [the sequined football jersey 1967], between function and luxury [the grey flannel dress with sable cuffs 1974], between masculine and feminine [lace in tandem with quilted men's shirting 1988]."

In the hands of this man who is a native of nowhere and everywhere, geographical borders also dissolve. Beene has been catapulting around the globe like a man shot out of a circus cannon since he was nineteen. He is fueled by a "compulsion for change," by "a fear of not flying." For him, there is no such thing as overexposure. Every indelible image from these faraway places is developed straight into the fiber, the fabric of his clothing.

"A Lesotho tribe recreated his sketches as a design motif on tapestry coats," notes critic Mary Lou Luthor. "[Just as] a chapel in the South of France with its Matisse mosaics later resurfaced as a print motif on a cloque from Spain." There are innumerable other assimilations in which the foreign is made familiar (and vice versa): from his religious devotion to the color black (Japan) to his fall 1984 "postcard" from Vienna. Subtitled "Horsing Around" by the designer, this allusion to the city's high-stepping Lippizaners features a black jersey and silk taffeta dress beneath a bolero made of a Hudson Bay blanket with lurex piping, Ultrasuede lining, and tiny rhinestone and jet buttons. As with so much of his work, it is a potentially combustible combination of materials in which the collision, the conflict between known and unknown, becomes inextricably one.

It's ironic, once again. Beene himself now lives in a borderless world — the world of on-line technology and MTV. It is a world which is as synonymous with connection as it is with collision and conflict. Unlike Beene's carefully constructed mosaics, his quick-cut collages of the exotically foreign and familiar that take flight in such mysteriously memorable ways, MTV's images, with their flash frames and jump cuts, their high-tech mutations and morphing, seem to crash into fragments on impact. Unlike Beene who also loves to startle and surprise the eye, to keep it traveling on anything but a straight line, the rapid eye movement of this new media leapfrogs from Moscow to Maine, from Prague to Paris and onto New York — all to return home as a form of white noise. Unlike Beene, it offers a tenuous hold, through remote control, on a world that is both one and the same.

Beene finds nothing to hold onto, no comfort, in a world that is one and the same. Sameness sucks the life out of form and leaves it inert and flat, without dimension or depth. "His clothes manage to contain that elusive but pleasing tension between movement and stillness, light and darkness, modesty and seduction," comments another reviewer. In Beene's world, it is that tension; it is the differences — the dissonance and the clash of contradictions — which create certainty and conviction.

A firm believer in what Livingstone describes as "the complex dynamism between the wearer and the worn"; in complicity, his clothes are supremely comfortable. Yet, again, he is an intensely uncomfortable man. For him, too much comfort implies going through the motions, "grabbing the hand of complacency." It is, metaphorically speaking, like settling for life in some suburb of diluted dreams and desires.

For those settlers who ache for a glimpse of a world which is bigger than that suburb, Geoffrey Beene opens up a new vista. "I have become boundless, unpredictable to myself, and multiple in possibilities . . . ." This is how Witold Gombrowitz sees that vista, that vision of flight and the "unfettered self." His statement expresses as much of a wish as it defines what is wanting in this on-line world of MTV and frequent flyers. It also happens to be the departure point from which all art begins its journey.

The Anatomy of Dress

"It is not we who speak the language, it is the language which speaks to us . . ."
Czelaw Milosz

Slide into the embrace, the caress which is Beene's concept of the dress. Only then can you grasp the meaning behind his words: "Clothes should look as if they haven't been born yet; as if a woman were born into them. It's a form of possession, this belonging of one to the other." Creating that bond, that oneness of being between body and cloth, represents both "destination" and journey for Geoffrey Beene.

He travels, he skims along the geography of its finished form with an almost hypnotic sense of purpose and ease. It is as if he has always yet never been here before. He is intrepid, curious, careful. He traces the path of a spiraling seam like some explorer eager to reveal his new route to the unknown, the unseen. From time to time, he stand backs, squints, and admires the view.

"You mold a woman into what you perceive her as being," he says. "What I do is the product of my admiration. I imagine women in an idyllic state. I create a vision of this woman, whether she exists or not. Doesn't every human aim for perfection? For the possibility of it?"

The myth of Pygmalion is a favorite of Beene's. The original Pygmalion was the King of Cyprus, a sculptor who carved a statue of the goddess Aphrodite from a piece of ivory. When he fell desperately in love with the image of his own perfection and desire, the gods took pity on him. They brought the statue to life. Pity, however, soon became a form of divine revenge. Unlike Beene, the fate that awaited Pygmalion and his work of art left quite a bit to be desired.

"An object demands of an artist an effort to go beyond himself," replies Beene. "For clothing is also language, a link between the creator and the wearer." When he speaks of that link, his language is emotional. It has zero to do with the bare bones of construction, with his bible of the body: Gray's Anatomy. "This one is full of apprehension and experience," he says circling

103

around a short dress in wool jersey. "I call it the Swallow. See the asymmetrical hem, how it flutters. And the shape of these wings in the back? I've clipped them by putting a pock-et here. I think it helps bring it back down to earth." He names another "the Clash of the Titans," then takes off and talks elatedly of those made of "mobiles, soft geometrical forms

which float about the body and surround it in tender spaciness."

He makes constant allusions to his eternal triangles, to the geometry of cubes, cones, and spheres and to the freeflowing movement of dancers and ath-letes. "My clothes don't need a label. I can tell they're mine just by how they move with a woman . . . ."

When others dissect his "body of ideas," the language is equally unexpect-ed: "Triumphs of a graphic will—strong and linear as drawings," says Vogue. "With clothes joined along seams that have the bravado of an orange peeled in one movement." "Like pure rarified poetry," says Bill Cunningham. "With gowns and dresses," says Paper, on which "laser guns appear to have sprayed slices of metal and beams of light."

This is language which is temporarily blind to the significance of missing buttons and side seams, to the vocabulary of his craft. It transcends the importance of signature piping and borders, the draping, insets, quilting, even the cut (which is as clean as a surgeon's). It's about getting into and under the skin—a purely visceral response to an object which might, otherwise, be perceived as inanimate, lifeless.

Like Pygmalion, Beene lives, he longs to give a third and physical dimension to his works of art, to clothing that embodies the heaven and hell of human desire. "Clothing is a crucial tool in seduction and yet constitutes the

ultimate obstacle to desire," writes Phillipe Perrot in Fashioning the Bourgeoisie. "It fulfills its erotic function best at the point where it gapes, tucks up, and acts as a potential brake, defense, or delay . . . ."

What ecstasy there is in that defense, that delay, and how profoundly Beene understands the beauty of manipulating it. How he revels in his role as "agent provocateur." He finds voluptuousness in virtue: in the modest nunlike front of a long black dress which turns to expose the erotic zone of an innocently bared back. He is calculating, devious in his use of the veil; with his layers of lace, voile, tulle, sheer jersey, and mesh; and of those twisted seams that undulate, snake, and wrap about the body. In his very grown-up version of hide-and-seek, every possible body part, from the nape of the neck, the bosom, and buttocks to the shoulders and fingers of a woman's hand, provoke some highly charged sense of erotic promise.

"A fundamentally modest man who is mainly concerned with designing for his pleasure and for the pleasure, for the 'sheer' pleasure, of others." This is how the man himself defines his calling. In his particular case, it is a pleasure in which passion governs all.

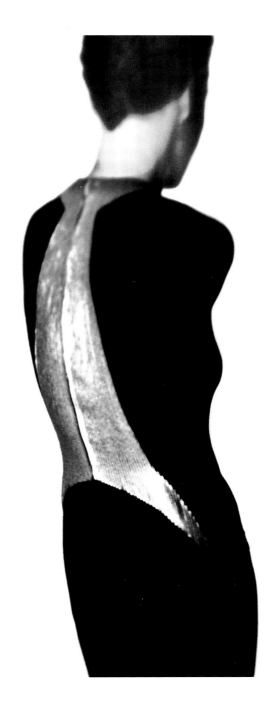

Beene to Beene

What's Beene Said

Oh yes, indeed. I've been called a lot of things other than Mr. Beene, believe me.

Dressing for success is something unsuccessful women do.

Anything tedious requiring road maps to put on is not my idea of modern.

What do I ask a model interested in working for me? Probably how well she does handsprings.

Beauty is a measure of energy.

I didn't leave the South. I fled. I'm still fleeing.

The issue of hemlines is absurd. If they continue to bring it up, the entire woman's movement will have been in vain.

We will always have the rich. Without the rich, we wouldn't know what poor was.

Yes, I believe most women will be wearing pants by the end of the century. And I sincerely hope I won't be there to see it.

The more you learn about clothing, the more you realize what must be taken away. Simplification becomes a very complicated process.

I used to loathe the idea of robots. But at least they perform perfectly. Unless a man screws it up.

No, I am not a citizen of the world. I am a nomad.

The zipper is on its way to extinction. It weighs too much.

125

Beene and the Body

I never met a woman in my life who did not have some beautiful part of the body. One nostril, skin texture, a fingernail, a toenail, who knows? The gift of a woman's body. The curves, the nape of the neck, the white shoulders. There is always wonderment. It's why I could never consider the body vulgar. The way it works, behaves, survives. It's just a miracle of God that we take for granted. A lesson in humanity.

Beene with Bias

Television? Television is the future but not the way it is now. Illiterate people with dirty fingernails selling fake stones. All those lounge lizards pushing buttons to buy that stuff, that junk. Assuming this country is going to be all right, and I believe it is, people will want something better. I just know it.

(As for trends). . . I do not wish to be clever or on the cutting edge. I hate trends. I have a compulsion to contest them. They manipulate. This is "In." This is "Out." It's ridiculous. I remember an editor once asked me to design a blazer. She said, "Geoffrey, you design me a blazer and I'll put it on the cover." Well, there never was a cover because there never was or will be a blazer.

Another editor came in. She was "into velvets" at the time, which is probably my least favorite fabric. Unless it's panne. She said to me, after I had shown her the entire collection, all these glorious fabrics, "So do you have any velvets?" Well, I had this pair of twelve-year-old velvet slippers I sent someone out to get. When they brought them in, I set them down before her eyes and said, There. This is the only velvet in the house.

I'll never forget the time either I wanted to make a coat the second time around and stores were saying, "Oh, no. This isn't new. This is last season." And I thought, My God! How can I dismiss the value, the pleasure of something simply because it is not brand new? Look at Chanel. She made that damn jacket thirty-five years ago and you're telling me I can't make the same coat the next season. I'm not listening to you. To hell with it. I just go ahead. Let my public decide and be the judge of it.

You have to stick your neck out. But oh! it's a tough business. Timing, timing is everything. When I first went to Italy in 1976, I was wearing these unconstructed jackets. I never felt comfortable in suits. Never. It was nothing but the merest semblance, the suggestion of a suit. I could move in it anyway I wished. Uomo Vogue was so impressed they did a spread on me. There I am in these jackets. Documented. The headline said, "Look out Italian Designers. This is the future." Hah.

I'll tell you the reason I didn't get more into menswear here which I love. I insisted that all that interlining, the padding, come out. It could not come out. The unions wouldn't permit it. The unions! A man gets paid every time that stuff is put in. They were protecting their jobs. Hindering modernism.

Here is another example that I simply do not understand. You can go to the moon but you can not make a synthetic fabric that behaves, that feels and breathes like the real thing. It's a brain block. Of course, even if they do invent it, they'll find a way to kill it. Dupont back in the 70s gave six designers in the world this yarn they invented. It was called Quiana. I gave it to Staron in Lyons. They made a synthetic satin velour out of it and it was exactly like the real thing. Except — and this was a brilliant except — it didn't wrinkle. I was astounded. But it cost too much to market to the masses and that was it. At this moment, the Costume Institute [at the Metropolitan Museum of Art] has it under lock and key somewhere.

I think the state of fashion at the moment is a mess. I do. I don't think that Europe is moving into the modern world with any ease or grace at all. It's bogged down in history. Why can't people be honest? America is still a young nation, we know more about how to cope and about how clothing ought to perform than anyone. It should be a time when American fashion shines. But big business is mostly what it is about these days. It can't afford to be other than what it is. It's confined, limited to what it can do for a price. It can't revolutionize anything.

Beene and the Inexplicable

I'm convinced there is a chemical reaction between the body and the mind. I wake up most mornings at 3:30. I'm ready to sketch. The moment I begin sketching, everything else in my life is out of my life. It's as though something glorious is happening. And it is. It's the only thing I have always been concerned with. The purity of that moment. There are no words for it. It has no explanation. People talk about ideas, inspiration, talent. It is simply that you seek out in your life what is that one thing that makes you feel whole. Something that is totally your own. And yet can be admired, understood by others . . . I'm forever grateful for it. It is being true to oneself. Just because I wish to express myself does not make me contrary. No. It's a question of standing by one's beliefs. I have no choice.

It is the reason I gave up medicine in the first place. I was asthmatic when I was a child. When I went into medicine and when I left I had to go into the army. The asthma became worse. They had to put me into the hospital. I had double pneumonia. I was going to die. Three weeks I was in there. And they finally came in and said, "Mr. Beene, you're discharged." I had said to the army doctor, I love design. I love clothes. He said, "Go. Go." So I went. I had my freedom. Once it happened and I left home, I never had asthma again in my life.

Freedom is the most costly thing on earth. I've said it before. So is exercising the fantasy. You have to earn the right to surrender to it. Sometimes the price you pay is unacceptance. By the press and the public. A friend, an editor, asked me recently, What are you up to?" My answer was "Frustration." It's constant. I'm always asking, "What can I do to advance, to go further? How much must I put into this to make the interaction of the clothing with the body and self more valid?" But the artist is also always working to protect himself. You are protected only for as long as you don't stop. By the measure of your work. Once you stop working, it ends. Life moves in. Doubt. Thinking too much . . . .

In the end, I am delighted that people cannot quite define my clothes. I'm not sure I can. Or I would want to. The clothes are their own mystery . . . the unknown, the intangible, the fascination.

A Chronology of Flight

1927 Born August 30 in Haynesville, Louisiana.

1943 Leaves Haynesville. Studies medicine at Tulane University, New Orleans.

1946 Confronts cadavers. Abandons medicine. Flees the South for Los Angeles. Forgoes University of Southern California. Works in display department of I. Magnin.

1947 Leaves Los Angeles for New York. Studies at Traphagan School of Fashion.

1948 Sails from New York to Paris. Enrolls at L'Ecole de la Chambre Syndicale d'Haute Couture. Attends L'Academie Julian.

1948-50 Apprentices with tailor who had worked for the couturier Captain Edward Molyneux.

1951 Leaves Paris. Returns to New York.

1951-54 Works for Mildred O'Quinn in Sherry Netherland Hotel. Drips mayonnaise on Louis XV-style chair. Fired. Moves onto other Seventh Avenue fashion houses with fewer fancy chairs.

1953-63 Designs for Teal Traina. Commutes to Rome between collections.

1963 Leaves Teal Traina. Launches Geoffrey Beene Inc.

1966 Flies in the face of convention: introduces menswear's own grey flannel and wool jersey into the ballroom.

1968 Waltzes sequined football gown into same ballrooms.

1969 Flies in the face of convention again: shows new men's collection together with womenswear.

1971 Launches Beenebag: one of America's first secondary clothing lines.

1972 Abandons heavy inner constructed clothing in favor of softer, free-flowing clothing.

1976-81 Packs up collection and flies to Milan. First American designer to show abroad. Follows up with shows in Rome, Paris, Brussels, Vienna.

1982 Sails to London. Returns. Terminates business relationship with partner. Defies menswear trend for women. Advocates short skirts.

1983 Takes off in new directions. Designs the golden-winged angel coat.

1988 Celebrates 25 years in business (and flight) with retrospectives across the country.

1989 Flees 550 Seventh Avenue: the mecca of American fashion. Opens the shop "Geoffrey Beene: His World" on Fifth Ave. and working atelier on 57th St.

1993 Runway runaway: deserts megamodels and traditional runway presentations for art installations.

1994-95 Celebrates thirty years of journeying with retrospective at New York's Fashion Institute of Technology. Moves to the form of dance. Stages performances of collections at New York's Equitable Center. Turns horsehair inside out and introduces it as a luxury fabric. In the space in between these events, Mr. Beene has been on the road, the sea, and in the air traveling everywhere from Italy, Japan, Spain, France, England, and Turkey to Mexico, Indonesia, the Island of Sylt, Hawaii, and Oyster Bay, Long Island. He has occasionally even returned to the land from which he originally fled.

Recognitions

1964 First Coty Award, First Cotton Council Award

1965 Neiman-Marcus Award

1966 Second Coty Award

1968 Third Coty Award

1969 Second Cotton Council Award

1974 Fourth Coty Award

1975 Fifth Coty Award

1977 Sixth Coty Award. His most meaningful. For giving
impetus to American fashion abroad

1981 Seventh Coty Award

1982 Eighth Coty Award

1986 Designer of the Year Award from the Council of
Fashion Designers of America

1987 Designer of the Year Award from the Council of
Fashion Designers of America

1988 Special Award for Fashion as Art from the Council
of Fashion Designers of America Young Designer
of the Year Award: Paper Magazine

1992 Honory Doctorate of Fine Arts Degree from the
Rhode Island School of Design

1993 Silver Slipper Award for exceptional creativity in
fashion from the Museum of Fine Arts, Houston,
Textile and Costume Institute

1994 "Geoffrey Beene/Unbound," 30-year retrospective
exhibition, The Museum at the Fashion Institute of
Technology, New York. First recipient of the Award
of Excellence given by the Costume Council of
the Los Angeles County Museum of Art. Scored first
in Creative Innovation and Long-term Value by
The Fashion Group

The Plates

Numbers preceding each entry refer to page numbers.

1 White silk crepe halter front jumpsuit; black silk crepe and leather mobile bolero. Spring 1995 [Photo, Andrew Eccles]

2-3 Black wool jersey halter and white silk crepe dress. Spring 1992 [Photo, Andrew Eccles]

4 Black and nude-colored sequin-embroidered silk chiffon body dress. Fall 1985 [Photo, Andrew Eccles]

5 Serpentine Dress: Black wool jersey and silver panne velvet evening dress. Fall 1986 [Photo, Andrew Eccles]

6-7 Black silk-and-wool charmeuse dress with gold silk-and-wool charmeuse body appliqué. Fall 1983 [Photo, Andrew Eccles]

8-9 Black wool crepe dress with wide leather belt. Fall 1967 [Photo, Andrew Eccles]

10-11 Taupe silk and rayon matte jersey dress with back-to-front stayed and released tucks. Fall 1975 [Photo, Andrew Eccles]

12 Black wool jersey evening dress with silk tulle inset back. Fall 1992 [Photo, Andrew Eccles]

13 Black wool and acrylic jersey backless evening dress with nude silk chiffon triangular insets outlined in silk charmeuse piping. Fall 1989 [Photo, Andrew Eccles]

14 Nude-colored double-faced wool crepe dress with black tulle insets. Spring 1995 [Photo, Andrew Eccles]

18 Greek Goddess: Olive-colored acrylic jersey body dress with undulating front yoke, small pleats, and open-back wrapped bodice. Spring 1986 [Photo, Andrew Eccles]

21 Jumpsuit with ivory linen pants and black rayon matte jersey top. Ivory and black-striped double-faced silk satin shrug. Spring 1993 [Photo, Peter Lindbergh, courtesy Harper's Bazaar, April 1993]

22 Saint and Sinner: Black wool jersey and white silk and wool hammered-satin evening dress. Fall 1988 [Photo, Guzman]

24 Gray rayon and acetate matte jersey evening dress with gray chiffon bodice and silver-sequined bustier. Spring 1989 [Photo, Guzman]

26 Taupe wool jersey jumpsuit; bittersweet brown leather jacket lined in taffeta. Fall 1987 [Photo, Guzman]

27 Dark gray wool and acrylic jersey pleated evening dress; multicolored double-faced plaid wool hooded bolero. Fall 1987 [Photo, Guzman]

29 Black silk crepe sportback jumpsuit. Spring 1989 [Photo, Guzman]

30 Brushstroke Dress: Yellow-printed black silk crepe evening dress. Spring 1964 [Photo, Robert Randall]

31 Red quilted cotton piqué one-piece day dress with white pseudo vest and black satin ribbon trim. c. 1963 [Photographer unknown]

32 From left to right: Black-and-white menswear worsted wool check two-piece dress with white silk blouse; black-and-white menswear worsted wool check dress with white silk blouse and black patent leather bow tie; black-and-white menswear worsted wool check dress with re-embroidered lace scallop cuffs and hem and black patent leather belt. Each, Spring 1968 [Photo, Robert Randall]

33 Gangsters, left to right: Black-and-white cotton jacquard suit; menswear-striped cotton suit with long jacket. Both, Spring 1968 [Photo, Robert Randall]

34 Apple green wool melton tent coat with elbow patches. Fall 1972 [Photo, Jack Deutsch]

35 Shocking pink double-faced wool gabardine day dress. Chartreuse satin lining. Spring 1967 [Photo, Jack Deutsch]

36-37 Football Jerseys: Pop art sequin-embroidered silk chiffon evening dresses. Fall 1967 [Photo, Hiro, courtesy Harper's Bazaar, September 1967]

38 Silk chiffon tank top evening dress with embroidered sequin Roman stripes and white ostrich feather trim. Designed for the Supremes. Spring 1968 [Photo, Jack Deutsch]

39 Black double-faced silk satin dress with inset trompe l'oeil white silk satin collar and cuffs and shocking pink tie. Fall 1971 [Photo, Jack Deutsch]

41 Orange double-faced mohair wool coat; wool jersey hooded jumpsuit. Fall 1992 [Photo, William Laxton]

42 Shocking pink and coral double-faced wool melton zipper front bolero; wool jersey hooded jumpsuit. Fall 1993 [Photo, William Laxton]

44-45 Left to right: Black linen jacket with white cotton asymmetrically buttoned triangular plastron; black silk piqué jacket with asymmetrical neckline and multicolored soutache trim; navy-and-white pin dot taffeta jacquard bolero with quilted navy-and-white cotton plastron; turquoise, red, orange, and yellow plaid silk taffeta jacket with asymmetrical neckline and matching soutache trim; navy double-faced linen jacket with asymmetrical neckline and nude faille trim; pistachio, turquoise, and pink plaid quilted silk jacket with quilted men's blue shirting plastron; black and ivory chalk-striped worsted wool full-length coat dress over white cotton T-shirt embroidered with "enfant terrible" motif; black and chrome yellow re-embroidered lace bolero with black chantilly lace scarf embroidered with wooden beads; multicolored striped silk gazar cardigan jacket with blue merrowed exterior seam detail; aqua ring-printed white silk faille jacket with rhinestone-centered frosted glass flower button. Each, Spring 1994 [Photo, Raymond Meier, courtesy New York Times Magazine, October 31, 1993]

46 Green-and-white striped cotton jacket quilted with silk taffeta; green silk taffeta skirt with navy silk taffeta petticoat edged in lace. Spring 1987 [Photo, Jack Deutsch]

47 Navy-and-white quilted cotton men's shirting bustier attached to double-faced wool gabardine skirt; navy blue double-faced wool gabardine bolero. Spring 1987 [Photo, Jack Deutsch]

49 Menswear look (detail): Taupe wool jersey dress with wrapped burgundy leather belt; navy blue double-faced wool melton coat. Fall 1982 [Photo, Jack Deutsch]

50 Detail: Black silk faille evening dress with brightly colored chenille dotted point d'esprit lace inset and sleeves. Fall 1989 [Photo, Jack Deutsch]

53 Evening dress with nude-colored cotton lace bodice and black silk tulle skirt embroidered with raffia over a nude silk charmeuse slip; black mesh scarf edged in chantilly lace. Spring 1986 [Photo, Alex Chatelain, courtesy British Vogue, March 1986]

54 Detail: Mohair wool plaid bolero with abstract sequin bead embroidery. Fall 1987 [Photo, Jack Deutsch]

55 Orange silk taffeta evening dress with polka dot-patterned sequins and bead-embroidered halter and point d'esprit inset at back; sleeveless bead-encrusted bolero with large red silk-embroidered flower. Spring 1991 [Photo, Skrebneski, courtesy Town & Country, May 1991]

56-57 Detail: White silk cloqué evening dress and silk faille bolero with pressed satin ribbon stitched in gold lined with cotton piqué floral print. Spring 1988 [Photo, Jack Deutsch]

58 Evening ensemble (detail): Black linen jacket with colored silk button embellished dot print; white cotton barathea waistcoat with cotton men's shirting bows and black silk buttons; "lifesaver" print faille skirt. Spring 1988 [Photo, Jack Deutsch]

59 Evening ensemble detail: Sequin-embroidered flowers appliquéd on quilted cotton faille bodice, quilted cotton faille jacket with multicolored jewel-encrusted buttons; silk faille gingham dress, striped cotton shirting bias trim. Spring 1988 [Photo, Jack Deutsch]

60 Double-faced gray mohair evening bolero with black sequin-embroidered falcon motif. Reverses to opposite colors. Fall 1989 [Photo, Jack Deutsch]

61 Detail: Green silk ottoman vest with "eagle eye" motif embroidered in metallic gold and silver thread. Natural Persian lamb lining. Fall 1987 [Photo, Jack Deutsch]

62 Detail: White silk faille bolero, white silk cloqué dress with organza petticoat edged in white lace. White cotton gloves piped in silk satin. Spring 1988 [Photo, Jack Deutsch]

64 Multicolored striped quilted hooded evening jacket. Fall 1993 [Photo, William Laxton]

65 Multicolored iridescent quilted taffeta jacket with large gold paillettes. Fall 1991 [Photo, Jack Deutsch]

66 Black double-faced wool satin bolero; matte tomato red sequin-embroidered bustier with silk faille box-pleated skirt. Fall 1987 [Photo, Andrew Eccles]

67 Sheared orange dyed beaver bolero-style jacket. Fall 1989 [Photo, Timothy Greenfield-Sanders, courtesy Mirabella, November 1989]

68 Suit: Black wool jersey jacket with watch appliqué; striped worsted wool skirt with silver metallic lurex trim. Spring 1987 [Photo, Jack Deutsch]

70 Black reversible double-faced wool coat with quilted gold silk and wool charmeuse "wing" motif edged in gold lamé. Wing motif reverses to silver. Fall 1983 [Photo, Jack Deutsch]

71 Platinum gray wool and silk charmeuse dress with gold satin circle appliqués. Fall 1983 [Photo, Jack Deutsch]

72 Black reversible double-faced wool melton evening bolero with copper front and hunter green sleeve of quilted silk and wool charmeuse motifs edged in gold lamé. Reverses to the same motifs in different colors. Fall 1983 [Photo, Jack Deutsch]

75 Ivory wool melton bolero with clear plastic tubing knotted at shoulders; black silk crepe dress. Fall 1994 [Photo, Jack Deutsch]

76 Black silk sponge crepe cocktail dress with black tulle inset; black tulle and horsehair "harness" vest. Spring 1995 [Photo, William Laxton]

77 Black silk gazar caban with white horsehair trim; black silk sponge crepe cocktail dress. Spring 1995 [Photo, William Laxton]

78-79 Black silk crepe jacket with cotton piqué tuxedo front and cuffs; black silk crepe pants. Spring 1987 [Photo, Hiro, courtesy Interview, May 1993]

80 Two-tone taupe silk jersey halter dress. Spring 1995 [Photo, Hiro]

81 Black silk jersey dress with black cotton piqué bra top. Spring 1995 [Photo, Hiro]

82 Blonde wool jersey V-back dress with twisted wrap shoulder ties. Spring 1995 [Photo, Hiro]

83 Black double-faced mohair wool jacket with rhinestone buttons; white double-faced silk satin harness-back vest. Rhinestone buttons. Fall 1993 [Photo, Andrew Eccles]

84 Black silk crepe dinner dress with black silk tulle "wings." Spring 1993 [Photo, Andrew Eccles]

86-87 Taupe ombréd triple-layered silk chiffon evening dress. Fall 1974 [Photo, Jack Deutsch]

88 Black wool and acrylic jersey single strap evening dress. Lace miniskirt not shown. Spring 1993 [Photo, William Laxton]

89 Black-and-white striped rayon dress with black jersey bra. Spring 1993 [Photo, William Laxton]

90 Brown and black "panther" print panne velvet dress with black spider flocked tulle evening coat. Fall 1994 [Photo, Jack Deutsch]

91 Black wool jersey dress with Lycra bustier and wrapped silver lamé cords; black silk tulle coat. Fall 1994 [Photo, Jack Deutsch]

92 Football Jersey 74: Pop art sequin-embroidered silk chiffon evening dress. Fall 1967 [Photo, Jack Deutsch]

93 Silk chiffon evening dress embroidered with sequins in environmental highway motif. Fall 1972 [Photo, Jack Deutsch]

94 Pistachio silk crepe evening dress with sequin-embroidered "Harold Teen." Spring 1971 [© Harold Teen; Photo, Jack Deutsch]

95 Detail: Yellow silk crepe evening dress with sequin-embroidered "Felix the Cat." Spring 1971 [© Felix the Cat; Photo, Jack Deutsch]

95 Detail: Blue silk crepe evening dress with sequin-embroidered "The Little King." Spring 1971 [© King Features; Photo, Jack Deutsch]

96 Red and black printed silk gold lamé and black silk sponge crepe evening dress. Fall 1991 [Photo, Jack Deutsch]

97 Black silk sponge crepe and overstitched blue panne velvet evening dress; matching bolero. Fall 1991 [Photo, Jack Deutsch]

99 Silk chiffon short evening dress embroidered with silver sequins with point d'esprit lace inset. Fall 1991 [Photo, Jack Deutsch]

100 Left: Black rayon matte jersey and silk crepe evening dress with silver lamé trapunto-stitched back and ties. Ties lined with black vinyl. Spring 1990 [Photo, Jack Deutsch]

100 Right: Silver lamé, silk faille "dalmation" print, and silver bound halter with rayon matte jersey full pleated skirt. Spring 1990 [Photo, Jack Deutsch]

101 Left: Black ankle-length silk taffeta evening dress with black-and-white sequin-embroidered circle motif; gloves with white sequined silk faille circle cuffs. Spring 1990 [Photo, Jack Deutsch]

101 Right: Black wool jersey T-back long-sleeved dress. Spring 1990 [Photo, Jack Deutsch]

102 Black wool and acrylic jersey dress with black leather harness. Fall 1993 [Photo, Hiro, courtesy Interview, May 1993]

104 Black wool and acrylic jersey evening dress with nude-colored silk chiffon insets. Fall 1989 [Photo, Jack Deutsch]

105 Detail: Long evening dress with black silk sponge crepe skirt; iridescent panne velvet and point d'esprit lace waist; half paillette-trimmed silk bodice with black sheer lurex trim. Fall 1991 [Photo, Jack Deutsch]

106 Black wool dress with black trellis lace insets and black floral appliqué. Fall 1991 [Photo, Jack Deutsch]

107 Black double-faced wool crepe dress with industrial zipper in front and re-embroidered black chantilly lace inset in back; silk crepe underskirt with black scallop-edged lace. Fall 1991 [Photo, Jack Deutsch]

108-9 Two views: Black and nude-colored silk jersey evening dress. Spring 1994 [Photo, Andrew Eccles]

110 Black silk crepe evening dress with stitched silver lamé insets. Spring 1990 [Photo, Guzman]

111 Two views: Black wool jersey evening dress with nude-colored sequin-embroidered silk crepe inset. Fall 1989 [Photo, Guzman]

112 Black silk crepe evening dress with nude silk chiffon inset. Fall 1989 [Photo, Guzman]

113 Black wool crepe evening dress; white silk faille vest with rhinestone buttons. Fall 1990 [Photo, Guzman]

114 Navy blue silk crepe halter-front jumpsuit and shrug with shoulder yoke and halter in white silk trapunto-stitched satin. Spring 1990 [Photo, Guzman]

115 Black wool jersey jumpsuit with brown leather "harness." Fall 1990 [Photo, Guzman]

117 Taupe silk jersey dress with plastic tubing at neckline and wrapping around waist. Plastic tubing sewn inside hem. Black double-faced wool crepe pants. Fall 1994 [Photo, Andrew Eccles]

118 Gray viscose matte jersey evening dress with chiffon front bodice and self-wrap sash. Fall 1984 [Photo, Steven Meisel]

119 Black evening dress from the Vienna-inspired collection: Black wool jersey bodice with black silk faille and multicolored silk and metallic ottoman drop-waisted full circle skirt. Fall 1984 [Photo, Steven Meisel]

120 Camel-colored double-faced wool melton coat with asymmetrical neckline and wrap closure. Fall 1993 [Photo, Andrew Eccles]

121 Cognac double-faced wool tweed coat with bouclé trimmed collar, cuffs, and placket, flattened by multiple stitching; cognac wool jersey dress with quilted wool and alpaca bouclé bra. Fall 1995 [Photo, Andrew Eccles]

122-23 Black/white double-faced reversible wool coat with black leather belt. Fall 1983 [Photo, Jack Deutsch]

124 Detail: Black double-faced wool crepe long full circle coat; matching hooded sleeveless vest. Chantilly lace mask. Fall 1993 [Photo, Hiro, courtesy Interview, May 1993]

127 Black double-faced wool crepe yoke-backed coat with wide black silk faille belt. Fall 1993 [Photo, Andrew Eccles]

128 Black wool jersey and silver silk jersey evening dress. Fall 1993 [Photo, Andrew Eccles]

130 Burnished gold and olive double-faced satin "naive" ballroom jumper with black silk T-shirt. Fall 1995 [Photo, Andrew Eccles]

131 White double-faced slipper satin "molded" dress suspended by wedge-shaped bodice and navy wool jersey sleeve. Fall 1995 [Photo, Andrew Eccles]

133 Gold-and-white iridescent silk organza wrapped evening bodice. Spring 1989 [Photo, Andrew Eccles]

135 Portrait of Geoffrey Beene. 1991 [Photo, Herb Ritts]

142-43 Black-and-white double-faced menswear tweed overblouse with black triple-flounce silk organza skirt. Fall 1995 [Photo, Andrew Eccles]

Front Endpaper. Black-and-white cotton gabardine suit with silk taffeta lining. Spring 1992 [Photo, Andrew Eccles]

Back Endpaper. Black wool jersey and horsehair bolero; black sponge silk crepe cocktail dress. Spring 1995 [Photo, Jack Deutsch]

Acknowledgments

To all the superb photographers, each with his own vision, my sincere appreciation: Alex Chatelain, Jack Deutsch, Andrew Eccles, Timothy Greenfield-Sanders, Guzman, Hiro, William Laxton, Peter Lindbergh, Raymond Meier, Steven Meisel, Robert Randall, Herb Ritts, Skrebneski.

Many persons have been helpful over the years and working on this project. In particular I would like to mention Dr. Christian Brandstätter, whose book The Apocalyptic Menu inspired my own; Mr. Leo Lerman, who first proposed the book; Mrs. Grace Mirabella Cahan and Mrs. Bernadine Morris, for giving me wings and clipping them appropriately; my staff, whose extraordinary talents materialized my ideas; Mr. John Dobkin, for celebrating my 25th anniversary at The National Academy of Design; Ms. Dorothy Twining Globus and Ms. Ellen Shanley, for unearthing the past to the future with the Fashion Institute of Technology retrospective of my work; and to my dachshunds, Maximillian and Sir Lancelot, who slept through it all.
— G.B.